Fifteen

(*Khamsata ʿAshara Maktūban*)

Shaikh ʿAbd Al-Qādir Al-Jīlānī

Translation and Commentary
Louay Fatoohi

Luna Plena Publishing, Birmingham, UK

Production Reference: 1100914

First published: September 2014

Published by:
Luna Plena Publishing
Birmingham, UK.
www.lunaplenapub.com

ISBN 978-1-906342-20-3

The cover was designed by Mawlid Design
www.mawliddesign.com.

Table of Contents

Acknowledgement

I would like to thank my brother Faiz who brought this masterpiece by Shaikh ʿAbd al-Qādir al-Jīlānī to my attention.

I am especially grateful to my dear wife Shetha al-Dargazelli for her helpful comments on the editing process and the translation.

I would also like to thank my close friend Tariq Chaudhry for his feedback on the translation.

My thanks also go to Kind Saud University and Michigan University for making their manuscripts of the book available online for public access, and to the Bodleian Library of Oxford University for providing me with a digital copy of its manuscript of the book.

The Author

Shaikh ʿAbd al-Qādir al-Jilānī was born in 470 H. (1077 CE). Old sources claim that he was born in "Gaylān" in the north of today's Iran.[1] But recently it has been suggested that he was in fact born in a village called "al-Jīl" near the city of Madāʾin 40 kilometers south of Baghdad.[2] That the current work was originally written in Persian seems to support the mainstream view that he came from Iran. Either way, this is why he is known as "al-Gaylānī," "al-Jīlānī," or "al-Jīlī."

Shaikh ʿAbd al-Qādir was born to very pious parents both of whom descended from Prophet Muhammad (prayer and peace be upon him). His father and mother are from the lineage of al-Imām al-Ḥasan and al-Imām al-Ḥusain, respectively. He received his first religious education at home before migrating to Baghdad at the age of eighteen to continue his learning and start what turned out to be a unique and amazing spiritual journey. References to only his mother advising him before he left his home town suggests that he had lost his father by the time he headed to Baghdad.

Baghdad was then the capital of the Abbasid caliphate and, more importantly, it was a center of knowledge and education that was vibrant with spiritual and intellectual activities. But this was also

---

[1] Al-Dhahabī, *Siyar Aʿlām al-Nubalāʾ*, vol. 20, p. 439

[2] Al-Gaylānī, *Al-Shaikh ʿAbd al-Qādir al-Gaylānī: Ruʾya Tārīkhiyya Muʿāṣira*, p. 9. Also, al-Gaylānī, *Jughrāfiyyat al-Bāz al-Ashhab*.

a period of political upheaval, with the crusaders in action in Palestine, Syria, and Antakya in Turkey, and Baghdad at the mercy of the neighboring Turkish and Seljuq Sultans.

In Baghdad, Shaikh 'Abd al-Qādir first accompanied the Sufi Shaikh Ḥammād al-Dabbās (d. 525/1131), and later Shaikh Abū Sa'īd al-Mukharramī (al-Makhzūmī). It has also been reported that Shaikh 'Abd al-Qādir was a student of al-Imām Muḥammad al-Ghazālī (d. 505/1111), and that the Shaikh's book *al-Ghunia* reflects influences by al-Ghazālī's *Iḥyā' 'Ulūm al-Dīn*.[3] He also had other teachers.[4]

When Shaikh Abū Sa'īd saw how his student was developing, he asked him in 521/1127 to teach in his school. Shaikh 'Abd al-Qādir used to lecture three days a week. His audience grew quickly until a lecture would attract tens of thousands. Many students used to write down his lectures, preserving the words of the Shaikh. He continued to preach in his school until his death in 561/1165.[5] The fame that this school developed as a result of the respect and following that Shaikh 'Abd al-Qādir had and its being his burial place guaranteed its status as one of the most revered and visited Islamic sites.

The Shaikh disapproved of the scholars and Shaikhs who built close ties with the rulers, visited them, or benefited from them, often at the cost of performing their religious duties properly. This is

---

[3] Al-Gaylānī, *Al-Shaikh 'Abd al-Qādir al-Gaylānī*, p. 12.

[4] Al-Dhahabī, *Siyar A'lām al-Nubalā'*, vol. 20, p. 443.

[5] Al-Dhahabī, *Tarīkh al-Islām wa-Wafiyyāt al-Mashāhīr wal-A'lām*, pp. 86-100.

what he says in one of his sermons:

> O backslider, you build relations with the sultans, the princes, and the rich seeking power and further worldly things, yet you do not do business with the King of kings, the Wealthiest of the wealthy, the One who never dies, the One who never becomes poor, the One who repays your loan to Him multiplied manifold![6]

Nobilities and rulers still attended his lectures, while he did not spare them any criticism he had of how they governed.

The Shaikh went for pilgrimage to Mecca twice, the first time in 505/1112, when he was still little known. In this trip he met Shaikh 'Udayy bin Musāfir (d. 557/1162). In his second in 555/1160 he met the famous Moroccan Shaikh Abū Midian (d. 594/1197). By then, Shaikh 'Abd al-Qādir had become one of the most, if not the most, famous Sufi Shaikhs, with countless followers everywhere. His mother, who had come to live in Baghdad, is said to have been with her son on his second pilgrimage. If this account is historical, then reports that his mother conceived him when she was sixty years old are probably incorrect.[7]

There is no figure in the history of Sufism who has been linked to as many miracles as Shaikh 'Abd al-Qādir. He is reported to have performed some miracles as one way to convey and support his teachings.

The influence of Shaikh 'Abd al-Qādir on Muslims and his role in the spread of Islam are

---

[6] Al-Jīlānī, *Purification of the Mind (Jilā' al-Khāṭir)*, p. 8.

[7] Al-Tāfidhī. *Qalā'id al-Jāwāhir*, p. 3.

impossible to exaggerate. There are far more Sufi Tarīqās (Ways) whose chains of masters trace themselves back to him than any other Shaikh. Accordingly, the followers of Qādirī Ṭarīqas far outnumber the followers of any other Ṭarīqa. Sufis in general and Qādirīs in particular played a major role in spreading Islam in Asia and Africa.

Shaikh 'Abd al-Qādir left a large number of sermons and writings. These include *al-Ghunia li-Ṭālibī Ṭarī al-Ḥaq, al-Fatḥ al-Rabbānī wal-Faiḍ al-Raḥmānī, Futūḥ al-Ghaib, Jilā' al-Khāṭir, Sir al-Asrār*, and many more. As noted earlier, while he authored a lot of works, some were compiled by his students who attended his lectures.

Let's read some of Shaikh 'Abd al-Qādir's words on a number of topics, starting with the following about love:

Woe to you! You claim to love Allah, yet you open up your hearts to others! Because Majnūn Laylā (the mad lover of Laylā) became truthful in his love for Laylā, his heart would not accept other than her. One day he came across some people who asked him: "Where have you come from?" He replied: "From being with Laylā." They asked him: "Where are you going?" He answered: "To Laylā."

Once the heart has become truthful in its love for Allah (mighty and glorified is He) it becomes like Moses (prayer and peace be on our Prophet and on him) about whom Allah (mighty and glorified is He) has said: "And We had caused him to refuse the wet-nurses" (28.12). Do not lie; you do not have two hearts but one, so once it Is filled with something there is no room for another. Allah (high is He) has said: "Allah has not made for any man two hearts in his breast" (33.4) — a heart that loves the Creator and a heart that loves the creatures. There can be no heart in which this world and the hereafter coexist.[8]

He said about trust:

O young man, religion in the sight of Allah is Islam, and the reality of Islam is surrender! You have to reach the state of Islam first and then fulfil surrender. Purify your outward by Islam and purify your inward by surrender.

Surrender yourselves to your Lord (mighty and glorified is He) and be satisfied with His management of your affairs. Give up your will and accept the destiny that your Lord (mighty and glorified is He) has decreed. Accept all of what destiny brings. Your Lord knows you better than you know yourselves. Accept His words with certitude. Receive His commandments and prohibitions with total acceptance. Receive His religion with all of your hearts, and make it your inner and outer covers.[9]

Here he criticizes the hypocrites:

Woe to you! How can you tell others to endure with patience when you are impatient? How can you tell him to give thanks in return for the favors when you have given up thankfulness? How can you tell him to be satisfied with the divine decree when you are dissatisfied? How can you tell him to renounce this world when you are full of desires about it? How can you tell him to yearn for the hereafter when you have renounced it? How can you tell him to trust Allah (mighty and glorified is He) when you have relied on other than Him? You are hated by the True One (mighty and glorified is He), the angels, and the hearts of the truthful and the righteous of His servants.[10]

This is how he encouraged spending on the poor:

---

[8] Al-Jīlānī, *Purification of the Mind (Jilā' al-Khāṭir)*, p. 16.

[9] Al-Jīlānī, *Purification of the Mind (Jilā' al-Khāṭir)*, p. 24.

[10] Al-Jīlānī, *Purification of the Mind (Jilā' al-Khāṭir)*, p. 36.

O miserable one, when a poor person comes asking for a loan, go ahead and lend him and never say: "Who is going to give me?" You must disagree with your lower self and give him a loan, and after a while make it a donation to him. Among the poor is one who disapproves of begging for alms, preferring to ask for a loan, with every intention of paying it back. He has confidence in Allah (mighty and glorified is He), and on the basis of this confidence he borrows. So, if he approaches you for a loan, O wealthy one, lend him and never face him with a request to pay back, for this would further humiliate him. If a long time passed without you receiving any repayment, go to see him, ask him to accept that loan as a gift, and absolve him of his obligation. Thus, you will be rewarded for his first joy [when you gave him the loan] and for his second one [when you turned the loan into a gift.] The Prophet (Allah's prayer and peace be on him) said: "A beggar at the door is a gift from Allah (mighty and glorified is He) to His servant."

Woe to you! How can the beggar not be a gift from Allah (mighty and glorified is He) when he takes from your share in this world to add to your share in the hereafter? He saves something for you that you will find when you need it. The amount that you give him will vanish and disappear anyway, yet on account of giving it to him you will be promoted by several degrees in the eyes of Allah (mighty and glorified is He).[11]

He said on good manners:

The Prophet (Allah's prayer and peace be on him) said: "Keep to good manners in your relationships with people so that when you are dead they pray for Allah to show mercy to you and when you are alive they yearn for you." Heed to this good advice. Tie it to your hearts and do not forget it. It points out to you an easy work that carries much reward. How good fine manners are! They are a source of comfort

---

[11] Al-Jīlānī, *Purification of the Mind (Jilā' al-Khāṭir)*, p. 106.

to the person who has them and to others. How detestable
are bad manners! They are a source of fatigue to the person
who has them and a source of harm to others.[12]

Finally, this is what he had to say about humility:

Be humble and do not be arrogant. Humility raises people
up, whereas arrogance brings them down. The Prophet
(Allah's prayer and peace be on him) said: "When someone
behaves with humility with Allah, Allah (mighty and
glorified is He) raises him up." Allah has some servants
who do righteous works that are as great as the mountains,
like the deeds of the predecessors, yet they humble
themselves to Allah and say: "We have done nothing that
can cause us to enter Paradise. If we would enter it, it
would be by the mercy of Allah (mighty and glorified is
He), and if He would deny us admission, it would be on
account of His justice." They continue to stand in His
company on the foot of bankruptcy.[13]

---

[12] Al-Jīlānī, *Purification of the Mind (Jilā' al-Khāṭir)*, p.
149.
[13] Al-Jīlānī, *Purification of the Mind (Jilā' al-Khāṭir)*, p.
157.

The Manuscripts

There are at least four manuscripts of this book. One is kept under classification "Hs.or.14314" in Databank der Orientalischen Handschriften der Staatsbibliothek zu Berlin, Berlin, Germany. The second is in King Saud University in Saudi Arabia, the third is in the Bodleian Library at Oxford University, UK, and the fourth is kept in the Special Collections Library at Michigan University, USA. In editing the book, I used the last three manuscripts as the Berlin manuscript was not available to me.[14]

King Saud University has made its manuscript, which we will refer to with the letter "S," available for public access on the University website.[15] It carries the classification number of "218 / khā' . jīm." The manuscript does not carry any title, but the classification information gives it the title of "*Khamsat ʿAshar Maktūban lil-Jilānī* (Fifteen Letters by al-Jilānī)". It mentions no date.

The manuscript is 17.5x25 cm and consists of eighteen folios each containing two pages, except the first and last folios each of which has one page. The first two pages contain an introduction to the

---

[14] I will use the term "book" or "work" to refer to the fifteen letters of Shaikh ʿAbd al-Qādir al-Jilānī. Each of the three manuscripts I used as a source for the letters contains a prelude and one of them has also an epilogue. These are clearly not written by the Shaikh, as will be seen when we review them.

[15] http://makhtota.ksu.edu.sa/browse/makhtota/2271/1#.U4Y x2 _ldX16.

work, so they are not part of the letters. The
introduction names the author of the letters as the
renowned Sufi Master Shaikh 'Abd al-Qādir al-
Jilānī. After praising the work, it states that the
book was originally written in Persian, before
identifying the translator as a certain statesman
called Sulaimān Ra'fat Pasha. He is said to have
made the translation after becoming a Governor
(*Wālī*) in Brūsā. The latter is today's Bursa, a city in
the north west of Turkey. The Ottomans captured it
from the Byzantines in 1326 CE and turned it into
their first major capital city between 1335 and 1413
CE. Having done some research, I could identify
one Ottoman Governor with this name, who became
Governor of Aleppo in 1852 for two years. He is
said to have liked scholars and writers.[16]

The last two pages name and commend the
sponsor of the copying and distribution of the
manuscript, as well as praises the author of the
manuscript. So the manuscript contains what
represents a "Prelude" and an "Epilogue" for the
letters. Both carry no any title and start with the
Basmala "In the name of Allah the Compassionate, the
Merciful."

The work itself occupies the remaining thirty four
pages. It consists of fifteen letters, hence the title
given to it. The first letter starts with the *Basmala*
but does not have any title. The remaining fourteen
letters do not start with the *Basmala* but each starts
with a title indicating the serial number of that
letter, such as "*al-Maktūb al-Thānī* (The Second

---

[16] Al-Bālī, *Nahr al-Dhahab fī Tārīkh Ḥalab*, p. 388.

Letter)". The words of the author are written in black whereas the verses are in red.

The Bodleian Library manuscript, henceforth "B," is one of thirty six manuscripts contained in one volume carrying the classification number "MS. Arab. c. 84" in that library. The manuscript is 12.2x30 cm and carries the title "*Al-Qawl al-Muṣīb fī Taʿrīb al-Makātīb al-Khamsa ʿAshar*" or "The Right Say in the Arabic Translation of the Fifteen Letters." The manuscript consists of three folios which are most of 6 recto through 8 recto. The second half of the last page contains an Arabic translation of a Persian text that has nothing to do with this book but is one of the other thirty five manuscripts that the volume contains. The copyist has put a line above every Qur'anic verse in the text.

Like King Saud University, Michigan University has made its manuscript available online.[17] This manuscript, henceforth "M," is part of a volume with the classification number "Isl. Ms. 257" that contains some of the works of Shaikh ʿAbd al-Qādir al-Jilānī. According to the last page of the volume, these works were collected by a Sufiān al-Wahbī al-Baghdādī at the command of ʿAlī Riḍā Pasha in Baghdad in 1257 H (1841 CE). The latter liberated Baghdad from the Mamluks in 1831 CE and returned it under the rule of the Ottomans. He then became the Governor of Iraq, Diyar Bakr, and Aleppo until 1842 CE when he was transferred to Syria.

---

[17] http://hdl.handle.net/2027/mdp.39015079126762.

The volume consists of 170 folios and 340 pages. The manuscript in question occupies 22 folios, from 11 recto to 32 verso. It is written in a clear and very beautiful script. The manuscript is 18.7x11.5 cm. Neither the volume nor the manuscript contains a title, but the copyist has used certain drawings to identify the beginning and end of each manuscript in the volume.

Each of manuscripts "B" and "M" starts with a short introduction. The two introductions are almost identical. Most of their text is found in the introduction of "S," but the latter has an extra text that does not exist in the other two. It looks to me that the additional paragraphs in the introduction of "S" were added later and that the text of the introductions of "B" and "M" is the original one. The original introduction may have been written by the translator of the Persian text of the letters, but it is more likely to have been added by one of the early copyists of the Arabic letters.

Apart from the extra text in "S," the main difference between "S" and the introductions of "B" and "M" is that these two attribute the translation to "the poor man ʿAlī bin Ḥusām al-Dīn who is known as ʿal-Muttaqī.'" The latter is a well-known scholar who was born in India in 885/1480. He lived in Medina and Mecca where he died in 975/1567. Although I have not had the opportunity to directly view the volume that contains manuscript "B," as I have only a digital copy of the manuscript, it looks from the information that I have managed to gather that each of the thirty six of that volume was either written or translated by Muttaqī.

While "S" has an epilogue that focuses on the sponsor of the copying and distribution of the manuscript, "B" and "M" do not have an epilogue. "M" concludes with the fifteenth letter, whereas in the case of "B" this letter is followed by a paragraph in which the copyist thanks God for enabling him to finish the work on the manuscript.

Manuscript "B" also differs from "S" in that every letter title is followed by a short description, something like a subtitle. For example, the title "The Second Letter" in "S" appears in "B" as "The Second Letter: On explaining strife and spiritual training and their fruit." It is clear that the brief description was not written by Shaikh ʿAbd al-Qādir but was added by the translator or a copyist as some kind of commentary. Nevertheless, I have included these descriptions in my translation. Unlike "S" and "B," the letters of "M" do not have any titles, such as "The Second Letter." The copyist has used a particular decorative design to identify the beginning of each letter.

It is clear that the three manuscripts represent three different copies of the same translation of the Persian text, as we shall see later when discussing the edited text. This means that it is not possible that the two claims of the manuscripts about the identity of the translator are true. It is highly likely that Muttaqī is the real translator of the book of Shaikh ʿAbd al-Qādir, as he is a well-known scholar with so many works. The attribution of the translation to the Ottoman ruler Sulaimān Raʾfat Pasha, who seems to have lived three centuries after Muttaqī, is wrong. Perhaps, this governor supported the copying of the manuscript like ʿAlī Riḍā Pasha.

Manuscript "S" - Page 1

Manuscript "S" - Page 2

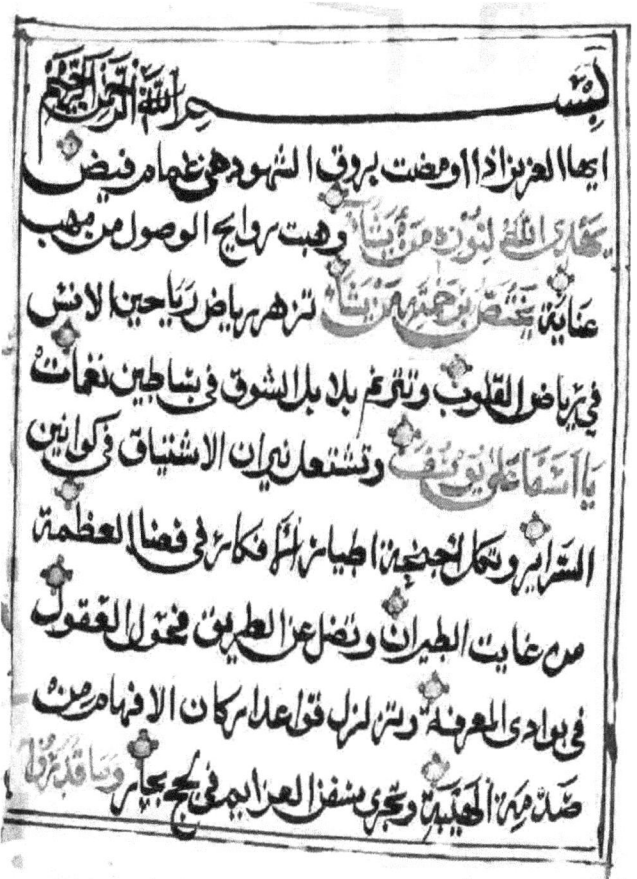

Manuscript "S" - Page 3

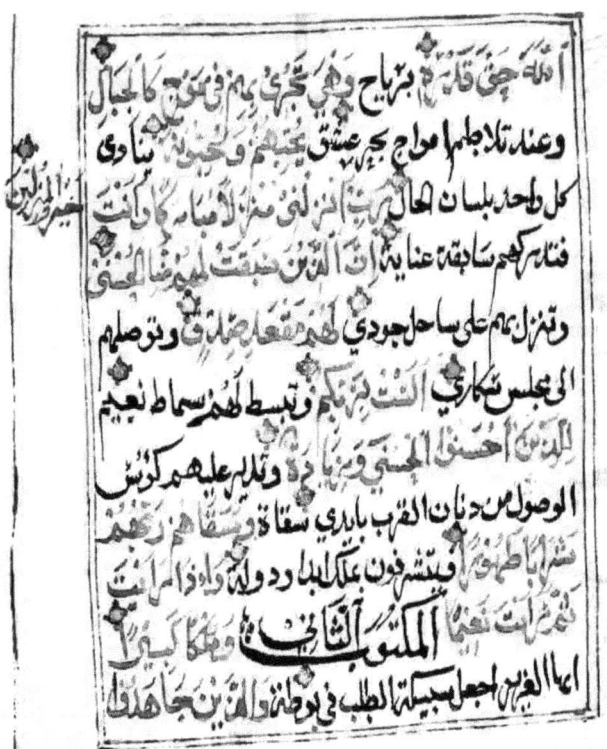

Manuscript "S" - Page 4

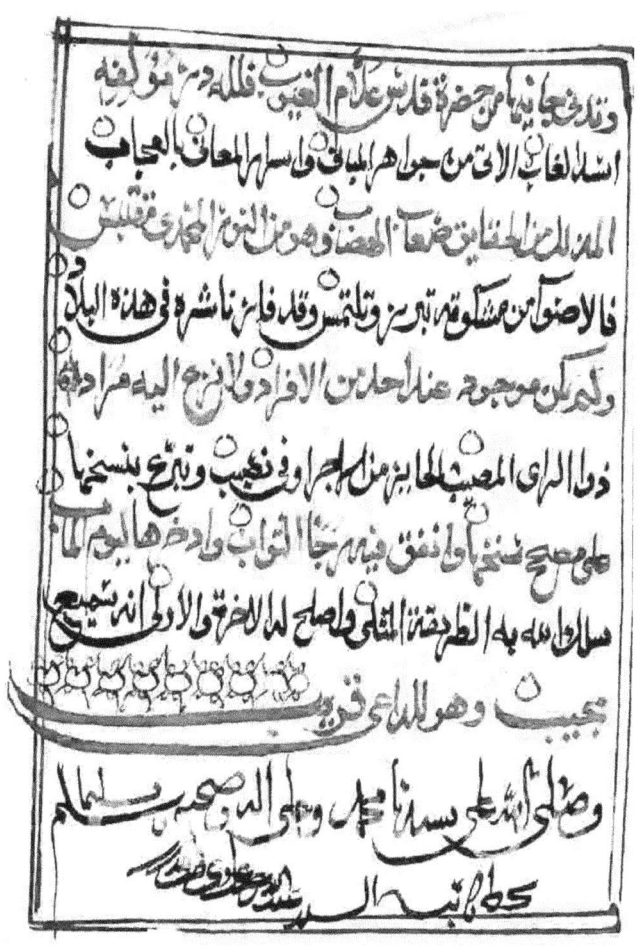

Manuscript "S" - Last Page

بِسْمِ اللهِ الرَّحْمَنِ الرَّحِيمِ

الْحَمْدُ لِلَّهِ رَبِّ الْعَالَمِينَ ٭ وَصَلَّى اللهُ عَلَى سَيِّدِنَا

مُحَمَّدٍ وَعَلَى آلِهِ وَصَحْبِهِ أَجْمَعِينَ ٭

فَهَذِهِ خَمْسَةَ عَشَرَ مَكْتُوبًا لِلْأُسْتَاذِ الْقُطْبِ

الرَّبَّانِيِّ وَالْغَوْثِ الصَّمَدَانِيِّ الشَّيْخِ عَبْدِ الْقَادِرِ

الْجِيلَانِيِّ قَدَّسَ اللهُ سِرَّهُ الْعَزِيزِ كَانَتْ بِلِسَانِ

الْعَجَمِ مُشْتَمِلَةً عَلَى حِكَمٍ وَمَوَاعِظَ بِأَنْوَاعِ

Manuscript "M" - Page 1

الاستعارة والتشبيه والاقتباس والتضمين
لنحو مايتين وخمسة وسبعين اية قرانية ومشيرة
الى اذواق الصوفية وحلا فسنح للفقير على ابن
حسام الدين الشهير بالمتقي ان اعربه واترجمه
مضمون المكتوب مع اعترافه بانه مزج البضاعة
في العبارات لاسيما في الترجمة اشارة امام

| أهل الاشارة | | وهو هذه |

ايها العزيز اذا اومضت بروق الشهود من
غمام فيض ● يهدى الله لنوره من يشاء ●
وهبت روايح الوصول من مهب عنايته ●
يختص برحمته من يشاء ● تزهر رياحين الانس

Manuscript "M" - Page 2

في رياضِ القُلوبِ ● وتَتَرَنَّمُ بَلابِلُ الشَّوقِ في

سَباتِينِ الارواح بِنَغَماتٍ ● ياَ اَسَفِي عَلى يوسُفَ

وَتَشْتَعِلُ نيرانُ الاشتِياقِ في كَوانينِ السَّرائِر

وَتَكِلُّ اَجْنِحَةُ اَطيارِ الافكارِ في فَضاءِ العَظَمَةِ

مِن غايَةِ الطَّيَرانِ وتَضِلُّ عَنِ الطَّريقِ فُحولُ العُقولِ

في بَوادِى المَعرِفَةِ ● وتَتَزَلْزَلُ قَواعِدُ اَركانِ

الافْهامِ مِن صَدمَةِ الهَيبَةِ ● وتَجرى سُفُنُ

العَزائمِ في لُجَجِ بِحارٍ ● وماقَدَّرُوا اللهَ حَقَّ قَدْرِهِ

بِرياحٍ ● وهِى تَجرى بِهِمْ في مَوجٍ كَالجِبالِ

وعِندَ تَلاطُمِ اَمواجِ بَحْرِ عِشقٍ ● يُحِبُّهُمْ وَ

يُحِبُّونَهُ ● يُنادى كُلُّ واحِدٍ بِلِسانِ الحالِ ●

Manuscript "M" - Page 3

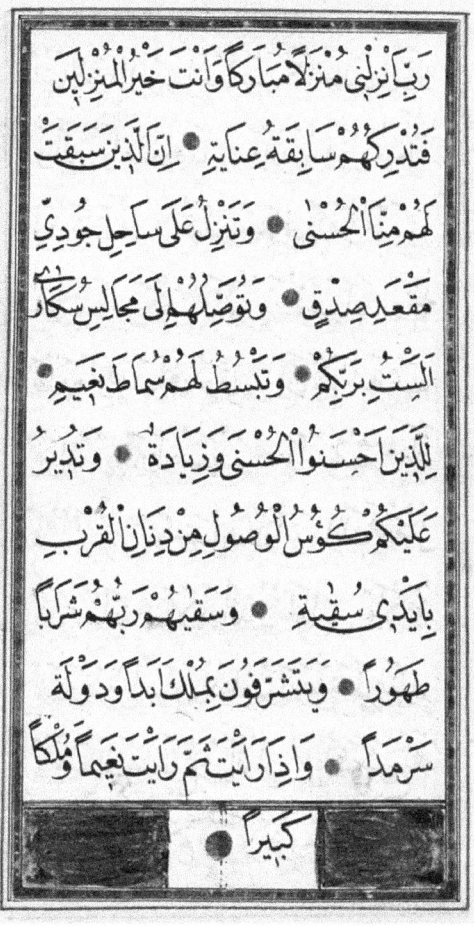

Manuscript "M" - Page 4

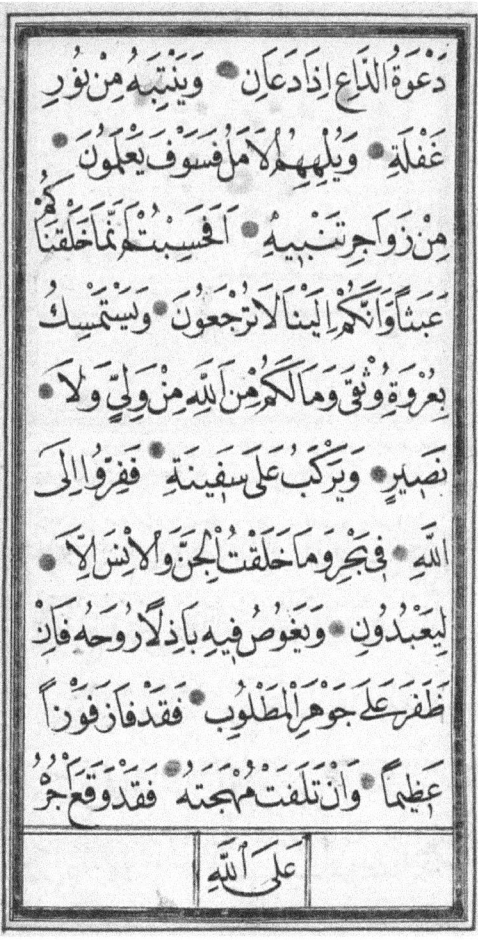

Manuscript "M" - Last Page

The Letters

With the exception of the second letter in "M," which starts with the expression "O dear servant (*ayyuhā al-ʿabd al-ʿazīz*)," and the thirteen letter in "B," which starts with "O brother (*ayyuhā al-akh*)," both of which look to be copying mistakes, every letter starts with the addressing formula of "O dear one (*ayyuhā al-ʿazīz*)". This is reminiscent of the expression "O young man (*yā ghulām*)" which Shaikh ʿAbd al-Qādir often used in his lectures.[18] These two forms address the listener or reader in general and do not refer to a specific person.

Articulated in a highly mystical language, the letters describe spiritual experiences that are attained through striving against one's base desires and committed devotion to Allah. They are written in a peculiar style whereby each sentence or group of sentences is followed by a related Qur'anic text, which is often a part of a verse. For instance, the Shaikh may mention a state of bliss that the believer will receive and then follows his statement by a verse that talks about the bliss in paradise.

The Qur'an is quoted in 267 places in the fifteen letters. At times, more than one verse is quoted in a location, so in total 279 verses are quoted. Some verses occur more than once, making the number of unique verses in the text 225.

The text, in effect, is a Sufi experiential

---

[18] See, for instance, his discourses in *Purification of the Mind (Jilā' al-Khāṭir)*, such as on p. 8.

interpretation of the quoted Qur'anic verses. This peculiar style of consistent pairing of mystical words of the Shaikh with a Qur'anic verse has produced an immensely beautiful text with a highly poetic tone. Often several pairings are connected with "and," which is a common practice in Arabic. This uniquely charming, poetic, and experiential way of interpreting the Qur'an forced me to put aside my other writing projects to edit an Arabic edition of the book and do this translation. It is something that I have immensely enjoyed doing.

The mystical language of Shaikh ʿAbd al-Qādir al-Jilānī speaks of spiritual experiences that words could do so much to describe, and the reader who has had no such experiences can at best hope to understand them only partially. This is why I have added a commentary to the text, but I have also kept it succinct and focused on my understanding of the main points of the text without any attempt to delve deeper into it. This should reduce the possibility of any misunderstanding that is likely to happen as a result of any further elaboration. I have not commented on any text that I found to be clear enough. Having been added as footnotes, the comments should not get into the way of reading the text alone without the commentary.

Any translation is an act of interpretation, so translating the Arabic text is in effect interpreting the understanding of the translator of that original Persian text. However, the fact that the words of the Shaikh consist of short sentences that are effectively interpreting clearly quoted Qur'anic verses makes it easier for the translator and limits the extent of any misunderstanding.

The Edited Text

There are some differences between the manuscripts, but it is clear that they are copies of the same translation of the Persian text. Such differences are expected to happen during the copying process. It is also obvious from the nature of the mistakes in the manuscripts that they have been copied from other copies. This is something that "S" acknowledges in its epilogue and "M" at the end of its volume, but there is no information about copying in "B."

In the Arabic edition of the book I compiled a listing of all differences between the three manuscripts. This is not of much use in the English translation so we did not include it here. In total, there are 180 differences between the manuscripts. Often two manuscripts would agree with each other and differ with the third, but there are a few cases where the three manuscripts each had its own version of the text.

Some of the differences are mere spelling mistakes or quite minor, like missing the Arabic letter that is equivalent to "and." But at times different words are used in the two texts and there are instances of words or even a whole clause missing from one of the manuscripts.

At times, it is clear which text represents the original, but at others this identification is not possible. In the case of the latter, I took a view on which version is more likely to be the original and used it in the edited text.

I have noticed that in most cases I preferred the text in "B" whereas the text of "M" had the largest number of differences with the chosen text. Of the 180 differences, the text of "B" agreed with my chosen text in 117 cases and differed in 63, "S" agreed in 85 cases and differed in 95, whereas "M" differed in 103 and agreed in 77.

I have added at the end of each verse the number of its sūra (chapter) and position there. These identification numbers are not given in the manuscripts. At times the quoted text occurs more than once in the Qur'an, but I have referenced only one of the occurrences, as I do not consider the broader context of the Qur'anic text to be relevant. In other words, I took it that the Shaikh always quoted the whole Qur'anic text that he considered relevant to what he was talking about, so the surrounding Qur'anic text of the quoted one is not related.

The text in "S" and "M" contains sings denoting the end of sentences, but there is no punctuation in "B." I have added punctuations to make the text easier to read. I have used square brackets to denote implied texts.

The English Translation

This is not the first English translation of this book. It was first translated in 1997 by Muhtar Holland, the outstanding translator of many of Shaikh ʿAbd al-Qādir's works into English. Mr Holland used the Berlin manuscript. It is clear from examining Holland's translation that the Berlin manuscript is closer to "B" than "S."

Translating a mystical work like this is a big challenge. The meaning of the text is often subtle, deep, and open to interpretation. The task of translation is not made any easier by the fact that the Arabic text is itself a translation from the original Persian. But as I explained earlier, the fact that the text consists of short sentences each followed by a Qur'anic verse makes the job of the translator easier. Unsurprisingly, Holland's translation and mine show differences in understanding various parts of the text.

The style of the writing has resulted in a translation structure like this: words of the Shaikh + of: + Qur'anic verse. I have used the character "—" to indicate that the text on a new line continues the preceding text. This is an example:

Be afraid of:
> The Day on which the person flees from his brother, mother, father, spouse, and sons, (80.34-36)

—and think of the reckoning of:
> Whether you show what inside your souls or hide it Allah will reckon with you for it. (2.284)

I have used "of" to link the Shaikh's words to the verse they precede, instead of using something like "that is mentioned in the following verse" which is too verbose. This means that the transition from the end of the Shaikh's words to the beginning of the verse is often not smooth linguistically but completely natural and elegant at the level of the meaning.

Each pair of words of the Shaikh and the verse that follows them has a concept that is present in both the Shaikh's words and the verse. The Shaikh's words explain the verse, and the verse explains what the Shaikh meant. So in the example above, the Shaikh is talking about a particular "call" that he quotes a specific verse to elucidate.

To retain the tone of the original text while at the same time presenting it in a way that is easy to read, I have put the long conjunctive sentences on separate lines. To make it easy to distinguish between the Qur'anic text and the Shaikh's words, I have used a different font for the former and placed each verse on a separate line.

Prelude (Manuscript "S")

In the name of Allah the Compassionate, the Merciful.

Praise be to Allah the Lord of all people, and prayer and peace be upon our master Muhammad and all of his family and companions.

These are fifteen letters by the master, God-supported pole, and permanent helper[19] Shaikh ʿAbd al-Qādir al-Jīlānī may Allah sanctify his innermost being. They include nuggets of wisdom and exhortations that use various kinds of allegory, similitude, quotation, and implication. They contain around two hundred and seventy five Qur'anic verses. They refer to spiritual experiences and states of the Sufis, embrace profound divine secrets, and advise the righteous followers of the noble Tarīqās. The truths of their edifices cannot be understood but by those who have spiritual knowledge, and the details of those truths cannot be reached except by those who have attained nearness to Allah.

Then someone with perfect intention deciphered the letters by translating them from their Persian origin to the gentle Arabic language, so that all wayfarers and seekers would benefit from them. After becoming Governor in Brūsā of the Ottoman Empire, the honorable expert and noble erudite Sulaimān Raʾfat Pāsha, May Allah endow him with

---

[19] "Quṭb (pole)" and "ghawth (helper)" are Sufi titles that represent specific spiritual positions.

whatever He wills, translated the letters into Arabic. May Allah reward the translator who has unveiled their meanings and uncovered the multiple interpretations of their words, so that their benefit would reach everyone of the saints and chosen. He translated the letters in eloquent expressions and effective phrases, including meaningful allusions and rhetorical and semantic devices. May Allah accept the effort of the translator for as long as this world and the spiritual world last. Amen.

May Allah's prayer be on our master Muhammad and his pure and goodly family, and May Allah have much peace on them until the Day of Judgment.

Prelude (Manuscript "B")

In the name of Allah the Compassionate, the Merciful.

Praise be to Allah the Lord of all people, and prayer and peace be upon our master Muhammad and all of his family and companions.

These are fifteen letters by the master, God-supported pole Shaikh ʿAbd al-Qādir al-Jīlānī may Allah sanctify his innermost being. They were written in the Persian language. They include nuggets of wisdom and exhortations that use various kinds of allegory, similitude, quotation, and implication. They contain around two hundred and seventy five Qur'anic verses. They refer to spiritual experiences and states of the Sufis may Allah be satisfied with all of them.

It became possible for the poor man ʿAlī bin Ḥusām al-Dīn who is known as 'al-Muttaqī to translate the letters it into Arabic. He acknowledges, however, that his ability of expression is poor, not least when it comes to interpreting the references of the leader of the people of references. This is the translation.

Prelude (Manuscript "M")

In the name of Allah the Compassionate, the Merciful.

Praise be to Allah the Lord of all people, and prayer and peace be upon our master Muhammad and all of his family and companions.

These are fifteen letters by the master, God-supported pole and permanent helper Shaikh ʿAbd al-Qādir al-Jīlānī may Allah sanctify his innermost being. They were written in the Persian language. They include nuggets of wisdom and exhortations that use various kinds of allegory, similitude, quotation, and implication. They contain around two hundred and seventy five Qurʾanic verses. They refer to spiritual experiences and states of the Sufis.

It became possible for the poor man ʿAlī bin Ḥusām al-Dīn who is known as ʿal-Muttaqī to translate the letters it into Arabic. He acknowledges, however, that his ability of expression is poor, not least when it comes to interpreting the references of the leader of the people of references. This is the translation.

The First Letter

On the first and last stages of the attraction by the True One

O dear one!

When the lightnings of direct witnessing[20] flash from the clouds of the emanation of:

> Allah guides to His Light whom He wills, (24.35)

—and the winds of the union of love blow from the windward of the care of:

> He chooses for His mercy whom He wills,[21] (2.105)

—the fragrant plants of close rapport will flower in the gardens of the hearts,[22]

—and the nightingales of longing will chant in the orchards of the spirits with the tones of:

> Alas, my grief for Joseph! (12.84)

—and the fires of yearning will burn in the stoves of the innermost beings.[23]

---

[20] "*Shuhūd* (direct witnessing)" is a spiritual state in which the person has direct revelatory experiences.

[21] This and the previous verse emphasize that Allah chooses whom to grant this spiritual favor to.

[22] The flashes of direct witnessing and the whiffs of the union with the Lover are not permanent, but they leave the heart with the unique experience of intimate friendship.

[23] Having tasted intermittently that unparalleled experience, the heart now cannot stand the separation and wants that experience permanently. The pain of separation is reminiscent of prophet Jacob's pain when he lost his beloved son prophet Joseph. The term "*sirr* (innermost being)" denotes the deepest

The wings of the flying thoughts will become too tired in the space of greatness in its pursuit of the destination of the flight,

—the greatest minds will go astray in the deserts of spiritual knowledge,

—and the foundations of the cornerstones of understanding will shake from the shock of the majesty.[24]

The ships of determination will sail in the depths of the seas of:

> They did not value Allah as He should be valued[25] (39.67)

—by the winds of:

> As it floated on with them amid waves like mountains,[26] (11.42)

—and when the waves of the sea of the all-engrossing love of:

> He loves them and they love Him, (5.54)

—collide, everyone will call in the tongue of the spiritual state

---

and most secret part of man.

[24] "*ma'rifa* (spiritual knowledge)" is an experientially acquired spiritual form of knowledge that is beyond the comprehension of even the greatest brains. It is not something that can be attained or understood by reason but it can become accessible only to the sound heart. Spiritual knowledge is a fruit of piety: "And be pious toward Allah and Allah shall teach you" (2.282).

[25] But the seeker is determined to continue his pursuit of that intimate closeness to Allah, knowing that He is worthy of every effort, and being aware of and avoiding the failure of those who underestimated Allah.

[26] This journey of salvation is similar to that of prophet Noah, which Allah commanded him to make and subtly directed.

> O my Lord! Disembark me with a blessed
> disembarking, and you are the best to
> disembark.[27] (23.29)

So the predestined care of:

> They for whom We have preordained good
> things (21.101)

—will reach them, and it will disembark them on the shore of the Jūdī[28] of:

> A seat of truth.[29] (54.55)

It will take them to the assembly of the intoxicated of:

> Am I not your Lord? (7.172)

—it will spread for them the tablecloth of the feast of the bliss of:

> For those who do good there will be good and
> more, (10.26)

—and it will pass around to them the cups of attainment from the casks of nearness by the hands of the cupbearers of:

> And their Lord shall provide them with pure
> drink,[30] (76.21)

—so they will be honored with an everlasting kingdom and the sovereignty of:

> And if you look far you shall see bliss and a
> great kingdom.[31] (76.20)

---

[27] As he negotiates the difficulties of sailing in the sea of divine love, he prays to Allah to guide him to the shore of His acceptance.

[28] Exegetes think that "the Jūdī" is the name of the mountain on which Noah's arch settled.

[29] Allah will then land the seekers safely as He guided Noah's arch to the Jūdī.

[30] Allah then admits them into the company of those who are intoxicated with His love. They will be served unique food and drink that are available only to those who attain nearness to Him.

[31] This turn of fortune and honor from Allah will be everlasting.

The Second Letter

On explaining strife and spiritual training and their fruit

O dear one!

Put the ingot of the quest in the melting pot of:

> And those who make efforts in Our cause, (29.69)

—and melt it with the fire of:

> And Allah warns you of Himself, (3.30)

—it will become free of impurities and fitting for the minting die of:

> We shall guide them to Our ways.[32] (29.69)

Its value and worth in the market of:

> Allah has bought from the believers their persons and their wealth for the paradise (9.111)

—will increase. Make it your capital so that you will get the goods of:

> Allah's is the pure religion.[33] (39.3)

An enigmatic intimation of the secrets of "and the sincere ones are in great danger"[34] will be revealed

---

[32] The person's apparent quest for Allah is in reality contaminated with other goals. It needs purifying by struggling against the lower self and heeding Allah's warnings, and then the person will earn the guidance of Allah.

[33] This journey of purification makes the person's quest fitting for Allah's way. It is a process of selling one's self to Allah in return for paradise. When this happens, the person will reap the fruits of having a sincere and pure quest for Allah.

[34] This clause comes from a saying attributed to the Prophet:

to you,[35]

   —and a ray from the lights of:

> Is he whose breast Allah has expanded for Islam so that he is in light from his Lord[36] (39.22)

   —will flash for you.

   The sellers[37] of:

> Call on Me and I shall answer you (40.60)

   —will move in your heart, and you will ascend from the lowest level of:

> Say the substance of this world is very little, (4.77)

   —to the zenith of:

> The hereafter is better for the pious.[38] (4.77)

   You will smell the breeze of the nearness of:

> And We are closer to him than his jugular vein, (50.16)

"All scholars will die except those who put their knowledge to practice, and all practicing scholars will die except those who are sincere, and the sincere ones are in great danger." This saying was reported by Warrām Bin Abī Firās (d. 605/1208), *Tanbīh al-Khawāṭir Wa-Nuzhat al-Nawāẓir*, p. 320.

[35] One's sincerity, which is the cornerstone of success, will be tested and can be easily compromised. How this danger might materialize will be revealed to the person who is working on acquiring sincerity, to help him remain alert, cautious, and focused to succeed in his quest and to protect his sincerity.

[36] Because of this sincerity, Allah opens the servant's heart to Islam, and this in turn makes the servant supported with a guiding light from Allah.

[37] The word "sellers" seems to be a copying mistake.

[38] The heart keeps on hearing Allah's command to people to pray to Him and His declaration that He is sure to answer their calls. You will ascend from the lowly position of seeking the riches of this world to the high status of seeking the infinite blessings of the hereafter.

—so the tree of your heart will shake by it, and you will get rid of everything by the autumn gales of:

Say Allah then leave them, (6.91)

—in the orchard of the divestiture of:

And do not call with Allah another god.[39] (28.28)

The winds of the spring of:

They for whom We have preordained good things (21.101)

—will blow in your direction, and dense clouds of favor and the clouds of:

He elects for Himself whom He wills (42.13)

—will rain on you with abundant raindrops.[40]

So the land of the gardens of the heart will become verdant with the plants of:

And We taught him a knowledge from Us,[41] (18.65)

—the trees of the orchards of the spirits fructify with the fruits of:

The mercy of Allah is nigh to the righteous,[42] (7.56)

—and the fountains of attainment will flow in the valleys of the innermost being from the spring of:

---

[39] You will start to get near to Allah, and this nearness will make you get rid of all attachments so that you seek no other than Him. This is the true affirmation of the oneness of God.

[40] Then Allah's foreknowledge of you will come true: you have been one of His elect.

[41] The term "knowledge from Us" refers to a special spiritual knowledge known as "*ilm ladunnī*." I have explained this in my article "The Concept of '*ladun*' in the Qur'an."

[42] Allah will grant this sincere servant who has become near to Him special divine forms of knowledge and surround him with the benefits of His mercy.

> A fountain from which those who are brought close drink.[43] (83.28)

Then the herald of good tidings of the advent of the good of:

> That is the favor of Allah which He gives to whom He wills (62.4)

—will deliver the good tidings of:

> You shall have no fear nor shall you grieve, and you shall rejoice in the good tidings about Paradise that you had been promised,[44] (41.30)

—and Riḍwān[45] of the gardens of the bliss of:

> Allah is pleased with them and they are pleased with Him (98.8)

—will proclaim

> Eat and drink with healthy enjoyment, in recompense for your works.[46] (77.43)

---

[43] The innermost being of the attained seeker will continue to experience the attainment to Allah.

[44] Having achieved nearness to Allah, this seeker who has succeeded in his quest will be given the good news of entering paradise.

[45] According to extra-Qur'anic Islamic sources, Riḍwān is the keeper of paradise.

[46] In paradise, the person will be told that he has earned Allah's pleasure and he will feel fully pleased with Allah. He will have an eternal blissful life.

The Third Letter

On fear and hope and their fruit

O dear one!
Be afraid of:

> The Day on which the person flees from his brother, mother, father, spouse, and sons, (80.34-36)

—and think of the reckoning of:

> Whether you show what is inside your souls or hide it Allah will reckon with you for it.[47] (2.284)

Do not occupy yourself with the works of:

> Those are like livestock animals.[48] (7.179)

Lower your head in the watchfulness of:

> So remember Me and I shall remember you, (2.152)

—and open the eye of your heart[49] to directly

---

[47] You must fear the Day of Resurrection, when relatives and friends cannot help each other. Those who misled and deluded each other will be enemies on that day: "On that Day, the close friends will be enemies to one another, except the pious" (43.67). Your fear must be increased by the your realization that Allah is aware of any thought you have, word you utter, and action you make, even if you try to keep it secret, and that He will hold you accountable.

[48] Livestock animals only eat, reproduce, and sleep. They are not aware of much beyond their minute world, as they cannot understand much. Working to feed their master, they are also completely oblivious to the inevitable violent death that awaits them. But the heedless person is in an even worse position because he is on his way to hell and because he chose this fate unlike the livestock animals which do not choose their lives and ends. Do not be that heedless person!

witness

> Faces that shall be bright on that day, looking
> toward their Lord.[50] (75.22-23)

Remember the bliss of:

> Therein you shall have all that your souls
> desire and therein you shall have what you
> want, (41.31)

—so you may hear with the ear of your heart[51] the proclamation of:

> And Allah calls to the abode of peace, (10.25)

—and you may wake up from the sleep of the obliviousness of:

> The life of this world is but a play and a
> pastime.[52] (47.36)

You will walk on the foot of the head in seeking the grades of:

> And the foremost, the foremost, those are the
> ones brought near in the gardens of bliss,
> (56.10-12)

—and you will make the horse of your resoluteness run by the whip of determination, so the herald of good tidings of the acts of gentleness of:

> Allah is gentle with his servants (42.19)

---

[49] The "eye of the heart" is the person's "insight" which allows him to see what cannot be seen by the eye.

[50] You must close your senses to focus your heart on the remembrance of Allah, so that it will be ready to receive spiritual revelations.

[51] The expression "ear of the heart" refers to "listening" to what is being said and seriously considering it as opposed to only "hearing" it.

[52] Focusing and reflecting on the bliss of paradise, your heart will start hearing Allah's words and understand His commands. You will realize that the short life of this world is wasted by most people.

—may receive you with the plates of the gifts of:

> They will have the good tidings. (10.64)[53]

You will triumph with the troops of:

> Allah's are the hosts of the heavens and earth (48.4)

—over the enemies of:

> Satan is a manifest enemy for man. (12.5)

You will get rid of the net of the desires of:

> The self commands [the person] to commit evil,[54] (12.53)

—and there will appear on the tablet of your heart marks of subtle favors of the secrets of:

> And be pious toward Allah and Allah shall teach you.[55] (2.282)

The bird of your spirit will remember the stables of old, so it will fly in the space of:

> So follow the beaten paths of your Lord, (16.69)

—with the wings of longing, and you will harvest from the fruits of close rapport in the orchards of:

> Eat of all the fruits.[56] (16.69)

---

[53] This is a journey for the heart not body in which you as a seeker need to emulate the highest achieving of Allah's creation. By continuing to work hard and staying determined to reach your goal, a messenger carrying the good news will finally come to you: "Those who say 'Our Lord is Allah,' and then go straight, the angels descend on them [and say]: 'Do not fear or grieve, but receive the glad tidings of paradise which you were promised. We are your patrons in the life of this world and in the hereafter in which you shall have what your souls desire and you shall have what you call for" (41.30-31).

[54] Allah's troops in the heaven and earth will support you to defeat the soldiers of Satan. You will also triumph over your lower self.

[55] Your heart will have signs of the divine knowledge that it acquired by its piety.

[56] Driven by your longing to attain to Allah, you will follow

The mirror of your innermost being will be polished by flashes of the lights of manifestations, so the secret of:

> He causes the night to pass into the day (22.61)

—will be revealed to you.[57]

The garden of your heart will become verdant by the rains of the mercies of:

> And We send down from heaven blessed water by which we cause gardens and the harvest grain to grow, (50.9)

—so all of it will become like a guiding garden and you will understand the cryptic references of:

> And We revived with it a dead country.[58] (50.11)

The curtains of:

> And We removed your veil from you so your sight is piercing today (50.22)

—will be removed for you, so you will get engrossed in the perfection of direct witnessing.

At times, you will drown in the seas of the independence of:

---

the paths to Allah that He had set, until you reach you destination and achieve your goal.

[57] Having attained nearness to Allah, the lights of nearness will cleanse your innermost being of all impurities, in the same subtle way that night replaces day. It is possible that the original text cites instead the second part of the verse which talks about the passage of day into night, which would have been more in line with the Shaikh's words about the illumination of the innermost being, and that the translator from the Persian text made mistake when copying the Qur'anic text.

[58] Your dead heart will be given life, and it will learn how Allah creates life out of death: "He brings forth the living from the dead, and brings forth the dead from the living" (30.19).

> Allah is rich enough to be independent of all creatures, (29.6)

—at other times you will be bewildered in the entanglement of the sandstorms of the majesty of:

> Do they feel secure from Allah's devising? (7.99)

—and at other times, influenced by longing, you will chant like a nightingale in the orchard of glorification when the breeze of the gentleness of:

> And do not despair of Allah's mercy (12.87)

—blows.[59]

Because of the overwhelming excitements your voice will rise by the with the tones of:

> I smell the scent of Joseph; may you not disbelieve me! (12.94)

—so the enviers will blamingly say

> By Allah, you are still in your old error,[60] (12.95)

—but when they will see the impact of:

> He cast it on his face, so he regained his sight, (12.96)

—they will pray in supplication and powerlessness

---

[59] When you, the lover, is granted direct perception of Allah, you will move between the various spiritual experiences that the act of witnessing creates, such as being independent of all creatures, being amazed by the divine schemes, and feeling intoxicated by the overwhelming sense of Allah's mercy which must not be despaired of.

[60] Those who have not experienced the grace of direct witnessing and nearness to Allah reject as nonsense what you, as one who has arrived at the presence of Allah, have to say. They will ridicule you in the same way prophet Jacob was ridiculed when he said that he could smell the scent of Joseph who had disappeared about 20 years earlier after being taken away to a far, foreign land, Egypt.

> Ask forgiveness for our sins. We have certainly been sinners,[61] (12.97)

—and they will say in truthfulness and sincerity

> Allah has indeed preferred you over us, (12.91)

—whereas you will say in the station of intimate invocation

> My Lord! You have given me a share of kingship and taught me a share of the interpretation of talks. Originator of the heavens and the earth! You are my guardian in this world and the hereafter; make me die as a Muslim and join me with the righteous.[62] (12.101)

---

[61] But when they see the miraculous evidence of the person who became near to Allah, they will be forced to accept that they were wrong, just like Jacob's sons who had to accept that their father had truly smelt Joseph's scent when they saw the miracle of the restoration of his sight by Joseph's shirt.

[62] They will accept that what they used to ridicule was real favor that they had no knowledge of, and that he who had it was preferred by Allah over them. You, on the other hand, will continue to appreciate Allah's favor to you and acknowledge that the continuation of this favor remains up to Him.

The Fourth Letter

On encouraging driving away heedlessness and repenting from acts of disobedience

O dear one!

Being oblivious and being deluded by the life of this world are not signs of happiness.

Do you not hear with the ear of the heart the address of:

> Are you content with the life of this world instead of the hereafter? (9.38)

Do you not fear the admonishment of:

> Whoever is blind in this world will be blind in the hereafter and more astray from the way? (17.72)

Do you not reflect on the threat of:

> The reckoning of people is getting close yet they are turning away in obliviousness? (21.1)

Do you not remember the censure of:

> He who desires the harvest field of the hereafter, We shall give him increase in his harvest field; and He who desires the harvest field of this world, We shall give him of it, but he will have no share in the hereafter?[63] (42.20)

Do you not pay attention to warning of:

> As for he who transgressed and preferred the life of this world, hell will be the abode?

---

[63] This verse substantiates what the Shaikh says in his introductory statement in this letter, confirming that attaining success in this world is no true sign of success, which is measured instead by one's fortune in the hereafter.

(79.37-39)

How long more will you continue to be bewildered in the wilderness of obliviousness and shackled by the chains of lust?[64]

Enter the cell of:

Turn repentant to Allah, (66.8)

—and with that state of mind face in the direction of prayer in the mihrab of:

Turn back to Allah, (6.79)

—and say with the tongue of truthfulness and sincerity

I have turned my face to Him who originated the heavens and the earth as a monotheist, and I am not of the idolaters.[65] (39.54)

So that He may reveal to you the precious secrets of:

It is He who accepts the repentance of His servants and forgives the bad deeds, (42.25)

—from the treasuries of acts of gentleness of:

Allah is forgiving, merciful, (2.173)

—and the messenger of the care of:

Allah loves those who repent and He loves those who purify themselves.[66] (2.222)

—may give you the good tidings.

---

[64] Your failures to listen, fear, reflect, remember, and pay attention to what Allah has revealed are all forms of a state of obliviousness, which you cannot escape while chained by your desires.

[65] Your repentance to Allah is like abandoning everything you are used to, isolating yourself form your former surroundings, and entering into seclusion with Allah only. The state of sinfulness is the result of turning away from Allah, so repenting is a process of returning to Allah by moving in His direction.

[66] Repentance allows you to experience the subtle forms and meanings of Allah's forgiveness, mercy, and love.

You will ascend on the steps of:

> You raise up whom You will (3.26)

—and the advent of good will call out to you in the tongue of the spiritual state

> Those who said Allah is our Lord then go straight there will be no fear for them and they shall not grieve.[67] (46.13)

---

[67] Then you will also learn what it means for Allah to raise someone, making you ascend to the place of salvation where you experience no fear or grief.

The Fifth Letter

On the togetherness with Allah (Exalted is He)
and how His knowledge encompasses all things

O dear one!

When the suns of spiritual knowledge rise from
their rising points in the skies of the innermost
beings, the lands of the hearts will be illuminated by
the light of:

> And the earth shall shine with the light of its
> Lord, (39.69)

—and the covers of ignorance will be removed
from the insights of the intellects by the kohl of:

> So We removed your veil from you.[68] (50.22)

The eyes of the inner senses of understanding will
be bewildered by directly witnessing the flashes the
lights of holiness,

—and the passing thoughts will be amazed by the
revelation of the wonders of the secrets of the
spiritual world.[69]

The eruption of all-engrossing love will make you
become lost in the deserts of quest,

—so you will find close rapport in the places of

---

[68] Spiritual knowledge appears in the innermost being and
spreads from it to illuminate the heart. Without this spiritual
form of knowledge, the intellect would be in a state of
ignorance, regardless of how much other forms of knowledge
it may have.

[69] This spiritual revelation is beyond the apprehension of the
intellect and its reasoning ability. It will leave the intellect
bewildered and amazed.

nearness because of the overwhelming longing.[70]

The caller of:

> Allah is rich in favors to people (40.61)

—will proclaim

> And He is with you wherever you are. (57.4)

When he sees the secret of togetherness he will lose his existence in obedience of the command of:

> And do not take another god with Allah.[71] (51.51)

He will dive in the sea of the extinction of:

> You have nothing to do with the affair. (3.128)

—to obtain the pearl of affirming the oneness of God, but the waves of jealousy will throw him in the ocean of greatness.[72]

Every time he seeks the shore he will fall in bewilderment, so he will say

> My Lord, I have wronged myself so forgive me! (28.16)

—then the boats of the aids of the acts of the gentleness of:

> And We carried them on land and in the sea (17.70)

—will reach him and disembark him on the shore of gentleness of:

---

[70] Being overwhelmed by longing, you will be in a state whereby you cannot stop your quest to find your Beloved. You will find solace and intimacy only when you get to places of nearness to Him.

[71] A voice will guide the seeker and teach him the real meaning of the fact that Allah is with every creature wherever he maybe. He will then become extinct as he understands what it means to not have another God with Allah.

[72] As he continues to seek extinction to achieve the essence of affirming the oneness of God, He will further take the seeker away from himself and will show him His greatness.

We target with Our mercy whom we will.[73] (12.56)

They will hand him the keys to the treasuries of the secrets of:

He encompasses everything, (41.54)

—and show him the enigmatic intimations of:

And that to your Lord is the destination.[74] (53.42)

He will learn the meaning of:

So He revealed to His servant what He revealed, (53.10)

—and understand the sign of:

He has seen from the great signs of His Lord.[75] (53.18)

---

[73] His endless journey of affirming his extinction and recognizing only Allah's existence will make him at times unsure about the right course of action. But Allah will come to his help and gently guide him to certainty, showering him with His mercy.

[74] He will experience the true meaning of the fact that nothing escapes Allah's knowledge and control and he will recognize the signs indicating that Allah is our ultimate destination who will judge us.

[75] You will experience what it means to receive Allah's revelation and you will see His major miracles.

The Sixth Letter

On the all-conquering power of Allah (Exalted
is He), the obedience of the rebels of the lower
self to it, and the occurrence of the resurrection
of the spiritual wayfarer in this world

O dear one!

When the troops of the attractions of the care of:

He elects for Himself whom He wills (42.13)

—overcome the government of the hearts,

—they will humiliate and tame the aspirations of
the evil-commanding selves by the harness of the
spiritual training of:

And strive for Allah's cause as is His due,
(22.78)

—they will put the tyrants of the desires in the
prison of piety bound by the chains of strife,

—they will shackle the pharaohs of wishes with
the fetters of:

Obey Allah and the Messenger,[76] (47.33)

—they will educate the actions of the will and the
preferences by the discipline of:

Whoever commits evil shall be recompensed
accordingly. (4.123)

—and they will completely demolish the bad
innovations of the remnants and habits and the

---

[76] When Allah draws near whom He wishes, the divine
attraction confronts the person's lower self, which drives him
to evil, tames it through guiding it to good works, and curbs
all desires and vagaries. The person will have only wishes that
reflect his obedience to Allah and the Prophet.

foundations of confusion and calamities.[77]

The caller of the spiritual state will proclaim with the tongue of truthfulness

> When kings enter a town they ruin it and abase the mightiest of its people.[78] (27.34)

So when the courtyard of the hearts is cleared and purified of the contamination of the impurities of the turbidity of:

> Whoever seeks a religion other than Islam it will not be accepted from him, (3.85)

—the gardens of spirits are perfumed by the breezes of the subtle favors of:

> Whoever Allah guides is the guided one, (17.97)

—the surfaces of the pages of the innermost beings are livened by the precious writings of the subtle favors of:

> Those He wrote faith in their hearts, (58.22)

—and the lamp niche of the consciences that is enlightened by the flashes of lights of:

> And Allah will complete His light (61.8)

—becomes the mirror of the lightnings of the direct witnessing, then his spiritual state will be as in this description

> The day when the earth is replaced by

---

[77] The seeker's actions and wishes will be guided by his recognition that evil will be rewarded with evil. The divine attraction will destroy all bad habits that are in conflict with the behavior of the good predecessors and it will erase all causes of confusion between right and wrong.

[78] When Allah invades the self, He destroys its corrupt state and demotes the base desires, wishes, and drives that control it. What looks like on acts of demolishing, sabotage, and murder are in fact acts of construction, repair, and reviving.

another earth. [79] (14.48)

The foundations of longing will vanish like
    Scattered dust, (25.23)

—and the tongue of truthfulness will say
    And you see the mountains and think they are
    fixed, yet they pass away like the clouds.[80]
    (27.88)

Isrāfīl[81] of the all-engrossing love will blow the
trumpet of:
    And the Trumpet shall be blown, (50.20)

—until the unveiling of the secret of thunder of:
    And everyone in the heavens and on earth
    shall swoon.[82] (39.68)

But the herald of good tidings of the advent of the
good of:
    The greatest terror shall not grieve them
    (21.103)

—will reach them and help them,

—and he will invite them to the highest place of
    A seat of truth, (54.55)

—with good tidings of the satisfaction of:
    Good tidings for you today.[83] (57.12)

---

[79] When the heart is purified from all that deters its surrender to Allah, i.e. declare its embracement of Islam, the spirit enjoys the blessings of Allah's guidance, faith is engraved on the heart, and the conscience that is enlightened by Allah's light reflects and the light of the direct experience of Allah, one's spiritual state will completely change.

[80] Having attained to Allah, there will be no more longing.

[81] The Qur'an mentions the trumpet of the Day of Resurrection (e.g. 20.102), but extra-Qur'anic Islamic sources name Isrāfīl as the angel who will blow the trumpet.

[82] The all-engrossing love will overwhelm them almost to the point of death.

[83] At which point they will be given the news that they will suffer no fear or sorrow, and they will be invited to occupy

He will open for them the doors of the paradises of bliss and he will say to them

> Peace be on you, you are safe, so enter and live it in it forever, (39.73)

—and they will say

> Praise be to Allah who has made good His promise to us and made us inherit the earth living in paradise wherever we like. How excellent is the reward of the workers![84] (39.74)

---

their places in paradise.

[84] They will be welcome into paradise forever, and they will acknowledge Allah's favor to them.

The Seventh Letter

On renunciation and its fruit

O dear one!

Go past the world of the delusion of:

> Let the life of this world not delude you and let not the Deluder delude you as to Allah, (31.33)

—and remember the stations of the people of awareness[85] of:

> You will recognize on their faces the radiancy of bliss.[86] (83.24)

You may smell with the nostrils of your heart a scent from the whiffs of the orchard of:

> His shall be repose, fragrant plants, and a garden of bliss, (56.89)

—and you may drink a gulp from the cup of:

> They shall be given to drink a sealed nectar whose seal is musk, (83.25-26)

—and the details of the secrets of:

> The truth has come from your Lord (10.94)

—may be revealed to you,

—while you are sat on the mat of the affirmation of the oneness of:

> Do not call beside Allah that which cannot

---

[85] "Ḥuḍūr (awareness)" is a spiritual station whereby the person is always aware of Allah.

[86] Ignore this transient world that looks misleadingly permanent and focus your attention on the next eternal world. Seek an abode in the paradise and aim to be one of those whose faces will be radiant because of Allah's bliss by acquiring permanent awareness of Allah.

benefit you or harm you.[87] (10.106)

You will hear from a night entertainment speaker of the close rapport of:

> We narrate to you the best of narratives, (12.3)

—the night entertaining speech of:

> By the witness and the witnessed.[88] (85.3)

So at times you will be enraptured by the utmost longing, enjoying the tones of the address of:

> So bear good tidings to My servants who listen to the word and follow the best thereof, (39.17-18)

—at times you will lower your head contemplating in sorrow because of the impact of the majesty of:

> So be straight as you have been commanded, and those who repent with you, (11.112)

—at times you will hold the strong rope of:

> Hold fast to the rope of Allah together (3.103)

—at times you will clinch to the hanger of:

> Victory is only from Allah, (3.126)

—and at times you will drown in the sea of:

> We will draw them in little by little from they do not know, (7.182)

—and at times you will seek refuge in the shore of:

---

[87] Then while you are still in this world, you will come to experience blessings of paradise, and you will understand the hidden meanings of having the truth from Allah. This will happen to you as a result of your affirmation of the oneness of God.

[88] You will have someone who will entertain you in your long nights of worship with stories from the unseen world, and the secret of direct witnessing and being witnessed will be revealed to you.

Allah is kind, merciful to you.[89] (57.9)

You will harvest from the gardens of:

Then he who hopes to meet his Lord (18.110)

—the fruits of:

Let him work a righteous work, (18.110)

—and you will scoop by the hands of sincerity from the rivers of:

Each will have grades according to what they did, (46.19)

—in the shade of the lote tree[90] of:

My prayers, devotion, life, and death belong to God, the Lord of the worlds.[91] (6.162)

You will help yourself to the feast of the bliss of

And who is more faithful to His covenant than Allah? So rejoice in the bargain you have made, (9.111)

—and you will hear from the caller of favor the proclamation

O my servants! There is no fear for you today

---

[89] You will experience various states: longing will make you intoxicated by the knowledge of the good tidings to those who follow Allah's words; a deep sense of sorrow will overtake you as you contemplate what it means to follow the divine command to be upright; you will hold firmly to Allah while resisting the trials that target taking you away from Him; you will wait in patience for Allah's help as you experience setbacks; you will experience bouts of fear that Allah may allure you away from Him while you are unaware; and you will find yourself saved by Allah's mercy and kindness.

[90] This tree is mentioned in the Qur'an in a set of verses (53.1-18) that are thought to talk about Prophet Muhammad's night journey and ascension to heaven, so it belongs to that spiritual world.

[91] Your hope to meet Allah will make you do good works, and you will have sincere devotion to Allah and complete surrender to Him.

nor shall you be grieved.[92] (43.68)

---

[92] You will enter paradise, enjoy its countless bounties and live forever with nothing to sadden or grieve you.

The Eighth Letter

On close rapport and its fruits

O dear one!

When the tone of the psalms of close rapport reaches the ears of the hearts, you will remember the pleasures of the tones of:

> Am I not your Lord? (7.172)

—and the states of intoxication of:

> They said "Yes."[93] (67.9)

The nightingale of sorrows will chant to the strings of the tone of the regret of:

> Alas, my grief for Joseph! (12.84)

—the oud[94] of griefs will sound with the tune of the heartbreak of:

> And his eyes became white because of the grief, for he was suppressing [grief], (12.84)

—and the mandolin of separation will play the sound of:

> I only complain of my grief and sorrow to Allah, (12.86)

—to the rhythm of:

> so, [my course is] perfect patience.[95] (12.83)

---

[93] When intimate closeness with Allah is attained, the heart will rediscover its state of affirmation of the oneness of God with which it was created.

[94] A musical string instrument similar to the lute.

[95] Having attained nearness to Allah, the person will suffer from any subsequent separation, in the same way that prophet Jacob suffered the pains of losing his son Joseph. But he knows that he only has to pray to Allah for the trials to go away, while bearing them in patience.

The lightnings of the attractions of longing will flash in the space of the skies of the innermost beings like the gleaming of:

> The brilliance of its lightning almost takes away the sight, (24.43)

—such that the insights of the eyes of the intellects will be extinguished,

—and the tears of grief will drop from the clouds of the eye of the spirits,

—so the lands of the farm of:

> He who desires the harvest field of the hereafter, We shall give him increase in his harvest field (42.20)

—will become verdant with the plants of:

> Allah has promised you many spoils.[96] (48.20)

The gardens of the hopes of:

> And he who relies on Allah, He is sufficient for him, (65.3)

—will be wholly perfumed by the whiffs of the scents of:

> Allah attains His purpose.[97] (65.3)

The branches of the trees of patience will, in sheer perfection, fructify with the fruits of:

> Those who are patient shall be paid without count, (39.10)

—and they will shake by the winds of the care of:

> This is Our gift so bestow or withhold without

---

[96] The longing for the Beloved that is initiated by the Beloved Himself will appear inside the lover. It is too wonderful for the intellect to deal with. Those tears of grief for the separation will be his medicine, brining rewards from Allah.

[97] He will reap the fruits of his reliance on Allah, leading him to the grace Allah had decreed for him.

account.[98] (38.39)

The caller of:

> And your Lord is the forgiving, full of mercy (18.58)

—will proclaim

> This is Our provision which shall never run out.[99] (38.54)

---

[98] The reward for patience, which Prophet Muhammad described as being "to faith like the head to the body," will be invaluable gifts from Allah.

[99] By His forgiveness and mercy, Allah will give him blessings that never run out.

The Ninth Letter

On promoting interest in the company of the good-doers and its fruits and renouncing the world

O dear one!

Turn away from the calls of the lusts of:

> And do not follow your desire lest it leads you astray from Allah's way, (38.26)

—abandon the places of the obliviousness of:

> And do not obey him whose heart we have made oblivious of Our remembrance, (18.28)

—and avoid the company of the people of hardened hearts of:

> So woe be to those whose hearts are hardened against the remembrance of Allah.[100] (39.22)

Hear with the ear of your heart the caller of:

> Respond to your Lord before there comes a Day from Allah that cannot be turned back (42.47)

—the proclamation of:

> Has not the time yet arrived for those who believe that their hearts should be humbled by

---

[100] Our personal weaknesses are one source of our vulnerability. But at least as significant is the influence others have on us. One is bound to acquire attributes from the people he accompanies. The company of those who are close to Allah and seek Him gets one closer to Him, whereas bad companions take the person further away from Him, hence the famous Sufi adage "choose the companion before you choose the way."

the remembrance of Allah?[101] (57.16)

Wake up from the sleep of the delusion of:

> Let not the Deluder delude you as to Allah,
> (35.5)

—by the warning of:

> Does man think he shall be left neglected?[102]
> (75.36)

Ask about the stations of the people of awareness of:

> Men whom neither trading nor selling distracts
> them from the remembrance of Allah, (24.37)

—and travel to the Kaʿba of the intended destination on the foot of the head in the desert of the devotion of:

> And devote yourself to Him with full devotion,
> (73.8)

—with the provision of divestiture of:

> Say "Allah" then leave them, (6.91)

—on a riding camel of the entrustment of:

> And I entrust my affair to Allah, (40.44)

—with the caravan of the people of truthfulness of:

> Be with the truthful.[103] (9.119)

Move away from the dwellings of the adornments

---

[101] Keep reminding yourself of Allah and be on your guards that your heart might lose the ability to respond to His remembrance.

[102] Wake up from your state of forgetfulness, for even if you forget Allah He will not forget you. He has created you with responsibilities, and He will hold you accountable and not neglect you.

[103] Study the way of life of the people of the remembrance of Allah and emulate them in journeying to Allah with complete commitment, getting rid of all attachments, and putting your full trust in Him. Make this journey in the company of devoted seekers.

of the world of:

> We have made all that is on the earth for an
> adornment for it, (18.7)

—keep a safe distance from the paths of the deadly ends of the temptations of:

> Your wealth and children are a temptation,
> (8.28)

—and move in the directions of the roads of the guidance of:

> This is a reminder so whoever wills let him
> take a way to his Lord.[104] (76.29)

Pray with the tongue of the desperate need of:

> Or who answers the person in desperate need
> when he calls on Him? (27.62)

—in supplication and powerlessness saying

> Guide us to the straight path,[105] (1.6)

—until the herald of good tidings of the ancient care of:

> Surely there is no fear on the friends of Allah
> nor shall they be grieved (10.62)

—receives you with good tidings of the greeting of:

> "Peace," a speech from a merciful Lord,
> (36.58)

—and carries you on the carrier of:

> Help from Allah and a speedy conquest,
> (61.13)

—and invites you to the paradises of the bliss of:

> They retired with a blessing from Allah and

---

[104] The journey will take you through various paths most of them are harmful to you so you must avoid them. Follow the road of guidance that takes you to your Lord.

[105] Acknowledge that on your own you will never be able to find the straight path that takes you to Allah, so continue to pray to Him to guide you to His way.

favor.[106] (3.174)

The breeze of the fragrance of the union of love will blow on you from all sides,

—and glasses of the drink of affection will be passed around by the hands of the cupbearers of the unseen, and the witness of direct witnessing will proclaim

This is your reward and your efforts have been appreciated, (76.22)

—and the caller of the close rapport will entertain in the night with the night entertainment speech of:

And Allah spoke to Moses, speaking.[107] (4.164)

He will expatiate on the statement of:

When his Lord manifested Himself to the mountain He made it dust, (7.143)

—so the vision of the eyes of insights will taste the intoxications of the states of:

And Moses fell down in a swoon, (7.143)

—and when they see the effects of the direct witnessing of:

Faces that shall be bright on that day, looking toward their Lords, (75.22-23)

—they will confess their powerlessness and say in the tongue of spiritual state

Vision cannot perceive Him but He perceives vision.[108] (6.103)

---

[106] Your sincere prayers will be answered and you will be given the good news of being brought near to Allah. Your abode in this world will be made like a small garden before the paradise of the hereafter.

[107] Having reached your Beloved, you will be rewarded with intoxication by the wine of divine love. You will be spoken to like those who enjoy intimate friendship with Allah.

[108] You will come to understand the meaning of Allah's

manifestation, and your eyes will experience direct perception. They will only be able to see the effects of divine manifestation, so they will concede the inability to see Him and affirm that He can see everything yet He can never be seen.

The Tenth Letter

On crying, powerlessness, supplication, and resorting to Him (Exalted is He)

O dear one!

If you do not put the forehead of desperate need on the dust of powerlessness,

—and do not make the clouds of the eyes rain tears of regret,

—the plants of your enrapture will not become verdant in the garden of life.[109]

The gardens of hope will not be pollinated according to what you wish,

—the branches of patience will not foliate with the leaves of contentment and the fragrant plants of close rapport,

—they will not fructify with the fruits of the nearness of:

> And he has a near place in Our presence and a good resort, (38.40)

—and they will not attain perfection.[110]

The nightingale of the heart will not chant the tone of longing,

—and the doves of your heart will not fly with the

---

[109] If you do not confess to your incapacity and dire need for His help and shed sincere tears of regret over what you have done, then you will not get any spiritual good.

[110] Without that acknowledgement of inadequacy and regret, you will not get what you had hoped for, your patience will not deliver any results, and you will not be brought near to Allah.

wings of:

> I am going to my Lord who will guide me,
> (37.99)

—from the cage of:

> Or shall man have whatever he wishes?[111]
> (53.24)

You will not cross the space of:

> Do not stretch your eyes to what we have
> given pairs of them — the flower of the life of
> this world — to try them with it, (20.131)

—you will not reach the lote tree of:

> In a seat of truth in the presence of a potent
> king, (54.55)

—and you will not reap the fruits of the trees of:

> They shall have what they wish with their
> Lord.[112] (39.34)

No breeze from the orchard of:

> With Allah is the best resort (3.14)

—will reach the nostrils of your heart,

—and your nose will not smell the scent of the flowers of:

> They will have their reward with their Lord
> (2.262)
> He is their patron for what they have done.[113]
> (6.127)

---

[111] You will not follow the way to Allah and escape from the traps of false wishes, and you will remain shackled to this world.

[112] You will keep your eyes on the worldly riches other have been given and you will fail to go beyond this world and journey toward the spiritual world. So you shall not benefit from Allah's promise to reward His sincere seekers with whatever they wish.

[113] Paradise and all spiritual benefits will be out of your reach without that necessary dedication to Allah.

The Eleventh Letter

On affirming the oneness of God and its fruit

O dear one!

When of the early signs of the light of the morning of affirming the oneness of God appear on the hearts from the eastern horizons of:

> And by the morning as it breathes, (81.18)

—and the suns of complete certitude settle on the constellations of the orbits of:

> And the sun runs to a place of rest for it, (36.38)

—the darknesses of human existence will disappear in the light of the flashes of:

> Their light running before them,[114] (66.8)

—and the secret of:

> He makes the night to enter into the day (57.6)

—will be revealed, and the veil will be removed from the face of Allah's predestined care of:

> Allah is the patron of those who believe, He brings them out of the darkness into the light.[115] (2.257)

---

[114] When the heart affirms the oneness of God and acquires the certainty of faith, the poor qualities of its human nature will vanish by the light of faith.

[115] The seeker will come to experience how Allah subtly changes him from his failed condition to the state that He wants, in the same way He can change anything from one state to its opposite, like His alternation of the night and day. He will see Allah's old ruling that He will lead the believers from the darkness of delusion to the light of guidance.

The troops of Satan of:

> Satan is an enemy for you, (35.6)

—will then launch an attack, in the battle of:

> So take him for an enemy, (35.6)

—aided by the soldiers of:

> The love of pleasures of women and children has been made to seem fair to people,[116] (3.14)

—against the troops of the heart who will say with the tongue of truthfulness and desperate need

> And my breast will be straitened and my tongue will not be fluent, (26.13)

—and they will pray in supplication and powerlessness

> And forgive us, pardon us, and have mercy on us. You are our patron, so give us victory over the unbelieving people.[117] (2.286)

The caller of:

> He has the keys of the unseen (6.59)

—will proclaim

> Do not waiver and do not grieve; you are the upper ones.[118] (3.139)

The help of the of troops of:

> And Our hosts will be the winners (37.173)

---

[116] Satan will then launch war against the Allah-seeking heart, calling on the support of the riches and attractions of this world, to try and dissuade it from following the path to Allah.

[117] The seeker will find the onslaught difficult and testing, but he will wisely realize that he is too weak to repel the attack of evil on his own, so he will turn to Allah and ask for His support and help.

[118] Testing the patience and devotion of the seeker, Allah will first reassure him with words of support and inspiration that he will come out victorious in this battle if he held his ground.

—will reach them, raising the flags of:

> When help comes from Allah and conquest, (110.1)

—and the vanguard of:

> We have given victory.[119] (48.1)

—will pull out the swords of:

> We will help our messengers and those who have believed, (40.51)

—from the sheaths of:

> We raise in degrees whomsoever We will, (12.76)

—and charge at the enemies, so there will be visible signs of:

> So they defeated them by Allah's permission.[120] (2.251)

The news of:

> Help from Allah and a speedy conquest (61.13)

—will keep coming, and the caller of the spiritual state will proclaim

> Say "Oh Allah, king of the kingdom! You give the kingdom to whom You will and You take away the kingdom from whom You will. You exalt whom You will and you abase whom You will. All good is in Your hand. You are powerful over everything.[121] (3.26)

---

[119] Having given the seeker the opportunity to successfully confirm his sincerity and the firmness of his faith in the unseen, Allah will then mobilize His own troops to defend His devoted servant against the two-pronged assault by the evil forces and the seeker's own frailties.

[120] Allah's intervention will ensure that his patient and firm servant is victorious in his confrontation with Satan and his lower self.

[121] The divinely aided servant will now continue to enjoy Allah's support and help, having firsthand experience of how Allah can promote and demote whom He wishes.

The Twelfth Letter

On encouraging the company of the good-doers

O dear one!

Exit the deadly end of:

> Wealth and children are an adornment of the life of this world, (18.46)

—and avoid the preoccupation of:

> Our wealth has kept us busy.[122] (48.11)

Raise the foot of your resoluteness from the lowest level of the company of those who are cut-off in the wilderness of the obliviousness of:

> They forgot Allah so He forgot them, (9.67)

—spur the horse of your quest to run in the field of all-engrossing love,[123]

—hit with the mallet of the help-seeking of:

> Seek the help of Allah, (7.128)

—the ball of the state of being in the lead of:

> And the foremost, the foremost, those are the ones brought near, (56.10-11)

—to the destination of:

> Those are on guidance from their Lord, and those are the prosperous.[124] (31.5)

So that the messenger of the sovereignty of:

---

[122] Your life in this world is a short stay in your journey, so do not mistake it for the destination. Stop being absorbed by the riches of this life to focus on the next one.

[123] Stop wasting your time in the company of those who are forgetful of Allah. Work hard in your quest for divine love, and seek the company of those who have drowned in His love.

[124] Rely on Allah in your efforts to join those who are in the lead of those whom He guided to Him and brought them near.

> And give good tidings to those who believe
> that they have a position of truthfulness with
> their Lord (10.2)

—may bring the good tidings of:

> Allah is kind, merciful to people, (22.62)

—and give you the unsealed document of the secrets of:

> Proofs have come to you from your Lord.[125]
> (6.104)

When you see the enigmatic indications of the hidden things you will rush with the foot of the head to the paths of safety of:

> This is the path of your Lord, straight, (6.126)

—you will head toward the park of:

> They will have gardens beneath which rivers
> flow, (2.25)

—and you will enquire about the eternity in the paradises of bliss of:

> They have with their Lord, grades,
> forgiveness, and generous provision.[126] (8.4)

The herald of good tidings of the care of:

> They for whom We have preordained good
> things (21.101)

—will reach you, and he will tell you about the kingdoms of the abode of peace of:

> Allah is pleased with them and they are
> pleased with Him, (98.8)

---

[125] Allah will then guide you, treat you mercifully and kindly, and reassure you with proofs that you are on the right path.

[126] Your understanding of Allah's signs and subtle language will further strengthen your determination to stay on His straight path. You will come close to paradise so you will start asking about the rewards of its inhabitants which you know of its existence but not its details.

—one by one, and he will invite you to the couch of:

> As for he who fulfils his pledge with Allah He shall give him a great reward, (48.10)

—and he will help you attain by the attainment of:

> You shall never attain goodness until you spend of what you love.[127] (3.92)

---

[127] You will then be told about all of the kingdoms of paradise, and you will be given great rewards for keeping your covenant with Allah and for spending in His cause things you loved and valued.

The Thirteenth Letter

On the indication of the verse "Allah is the light of the heavens and the earth," with reference to the secrets of other verses

O dear one!

When the flashes of the lights of:

> Allah is the light of the heavens and the earth (24.35)[128]

—shine on the lamp niche of the consciences, they cause the glass of the heart to be illuminated by the light of:

> The lamp is in a glass, the glass is as though it were a glittering star. (24.35)

The lightnings of the revelations of:

> Kindled from a blessed tree (24.35)

—will flash from the canopies of the clouds of:

> That is neither eastern nor western, (24.35)

—and ignite the lanterns of the concept of:

> Its oil would almost give light.[129] (24.35)

The secrets of the innermost beings will all be adorned with the stars of the ruling of:

> And by the star they are guided, (16.16)

—and with the stars of the ornamentation of:

---

[128] The first five statements and another three later in this letter quote different parts of one of the most allegorical and poetic verses in the Qur'an in which Allah describes His light, hence it is known as "the verse of light."

[129] When the person is exposed to divine light, it will enlighten his heart and allow him to experience secrets of that light that would be otherwise impossible to know or understand.

> We have adorned the lowest heaven with the
> adornment of the stars.[130] (37.6)

The moons of awareness will shine from the horizons of:

> Light upon light, (24.35)

—and ascend on the constellations of the ascension of:

> And as for the moon, We decreed stations for
> it,[131] (36.39)

—and the nights of the obliviousness of:

> And by the night as it covers, (92.1)

—will assume the quality of:

> And by the morning as it shines forth.[132] (92.2)

The fragrances of remembrance will exude from the bliss of:

> And those who seek forgiveness at predawns,
> (3.17)

—and the nightingales of the predawns of:

> Only little of the night they sleep, (51.17)

—will chant with the tones of sorrows and grief,[133]

---

[130] Allah's light will beautify the innermost being and provide it with guidance.

[131] Even though the seeker is still in this world which is for most people like a long night of unawareness, the light of Allah will give him a continuous state of awareness of Allah. His awareness will increase as he is promoted from one spiritual station to another.

[132] For this seeker, the temporary night that this world represents will become like the enteral day of the hereafter, as his state of obliviousness and forgetfulness is completely replaced with awareness, just like the day replaces the night.

[133] The seeker will spend most of the nighttime worshiping, and will pray at predawn to Allah for forgiveness. He is in a state of regret for all time lost away from Allah, and he is in sorrow because of his burning longing to meet his Beloved.

—so the morning of the sovereignty of:

> Allah guides to His Light whom He wills
> (24.35)

—will break, and the suns of spiritual knowledge will rise from the rising point of:

> He whom Allah guides is the guided.[134]
> (7.178)

The secrets of:

> The sun is never to catch up with the moon,
> neither does the night outstrip the day, each of
> them is swimming in an orbit (36.40)

—will be disclosed,

—and the subtle favors of the mysteries of the secrets of:

> And Allah strikes out parables for people, and
> Allah knows everything (24.35)

—will be revealed from the shapes of concealment.[135]

---

[134] Allah's guidance will be confirmed, and spiritual knowledge will be revealed to this guided seeker.

[135] As he observes how his night of forgetfulness and remoteness is changed into day of continued remembrance and nearness, the secret of how Allah changes the affairs of His servants and the world will start to be revealed to him. He will see in his own experience the practical meanings of Allah's general parables.

The Fourteenth Letter

On the perfection of spiritual knowledge, the perfection of religion, and their fruit

O dear one!

When the suns of the sky of spiritual knowledge reach the constellations of the perfection of:

> Today I have completed your religion for you, (5.3)

—and the tablet of affection with its full shine climbs on the ascending paths of:

> And perfected My favor on you, (5.3)

—the lightnings of the lights of:

> And I have approved Islam for your religion (5.3)

—will flash.[136]

The eye of certitude will witness the proofs of the effects of:

> Is he whose breast Allah has expanded for Islam, so he is in a light from his Lord? (39.22)

—in the great direct witnessing scenes of:

> The truth has come to you from your Lord.[137] (10.94)

It will see the truths hidden in the secrets of:

> Allah's are the treasuries of the heavens and

---

[136] When the experiential knowledge that the seeker receives is complete and divine affection continues to grow, then for him that marks the fulfilment of Allah's declaration that He had chosen Islam as the religion for people.

[137] Having attained certitude of faith, the seeker will experience the effects of being guided by Allah's light and he will live the meaning of having the truth from Allah.

earth, (63.7)

—and it will view the details of the truths of:

> And in the earth there are signs for those who are certain and in yourselves; do you not see? (51.20-21)

—and it will become a companion of the cryptic references of:

> And wherever you turn there is the face of Allah.[138] (2.115)

The winds of the emanation of:

> And we send the winds as pollinators (15.22)

—will blow, and the scents of the favor of:

> We target with Our mercy whom We will, (12.56)

—from the windward of:

> Allah is gentle with his servants, (42.19)

—in the orchards of:

> We will not waste the reward of him who does good works.[139] (18.30)

The trees of the gardens of:

> Allah is with the pious and who are good-doers (16.128)

—will foliate with the leaves of direct witnessing and bear the fruits of manifestation to the point of perfection.

The springs the attainment of:

> That is the favor of Allah which He gives to whom He wills (62.4)

---

[138] The seeker will know creatures of the heaven and the earth that are known only to Allah's elite. He will see hidden signs of Allah in himself and the world around him. His spiritual eyes will see Allah everywhere.

[139] It is Allah who chooses dead hearts to give them life, by virtue of His mercy to His servants. He then rewards those who appreciate and respond to His mercy in both this world and the hereafter.

—will flow from the high mountains of:

> And Allah is of the great favor, (62.4)

—into the riverbed of the valleys of the hearts.[140]

The caller of the unseen will inform on the tongues of creatures the news that

> Those who believe and do good works the Compassionate will give them love, (19.96)

—and the herald of good tidings of the advent of good will utter the good tidings of:

> O my servants! There is no fear for you today nor shall you be grieved![141] (43.68)

Satisfaction will reach them from the dwellings of:

> A good land and a forgiving Lord, (34.15)

—with the kindnesses of the greetings of:

> "Peace," a speech from a merciful Lord. (36.58)

It will open the feast of the satisfaction of the bliss of:

> Help from Allah and a speedy conquest, (61.13)

—and say

> Therein you shall have all that your souls desire and therein you shall have what you want, as hospitality from a forgiving, merciful One.[142] (41.31-32)

---

[140] With direct witnessing the seeker will experience how Allah is always with the pious. Allah's mercy and blessings will continue to come his way.

[141] It will be revealed to the accomplished seekers how Allah will give love to those who have faith and do good works, and they will be reassured that no grief or fear would inflict them anymore, and they will live in permanent peace.

[142] Allah will shower them with His satisfaction and peace, and He will reward them with the privilege of having anything they wish.

The Fifteenth Letter

On the benefits of the sound heart, the complete mind, and the truthful certitude[143]

O dear one!

It is necessary to have a sound heart that understands the enigmatic indications of:

> Therefore take heed, O you who have eyes! (59.2)

—a whole mind that comprehends the details of the secrets of:

> We will show them Our signs in the horizons and in themselves, (41.53)

—and truthful certitude that sees with the eye of the heart the proofs of knowing

> There is nothing that does not glorify Him but you don't understand their glorification.[144] (17.44)

He must receive with his heart the callers of the attainment of:

> And when My servants ask you about Me, then verily I am near to answer the call of the caller when he calls on Me, (2.186)

—and wake up from the sleep of the obliviousness of:

---

[143] The word for "certitude" appears in manuscript B by a copying mistake as the word for "oath," as clear from the text of the letter.

[144] The seeker must purify his heart so that he can fully understand Allah's exhortations and see how everything praises Him in its own way. He must focus his mind to recognize the signs in himself and around him.

And hope will distract them but they shall know, (15.3)

—by the rebukes of the warning of:

Do you think We created you without purpose and that you would not return to Us?[145] (23.115)

He must hold fast to the strong handle of:

And you do not have a friend or helper besides Allah, (42.31)

—and board the ship of:

So flee to Allah, (51.50)

—in the sea of knowing

I have not created the jinn and mankind but to worship Me, (51.56)

—and he must dive in it risking his life.[146]

If he then obtains the sought pearl then

He has triumphed a great triumph, (33.71)

—and if he dies then

His wage shall fall on Allah.[147] (4.100)

---

[145] His heart must firmly believe that Allah is near to him and ready to answer his prayers, he must not allow anything to distract him from his Lord, and he should never forget that he was created for a purpose.

[146] He must always affirm the oneness of God, see Allah and Allah alone, and remember that he was created in order to worship Allah and get near to Him.

[147] He must risk everything, including his life, in seeking Allah. If he attains what he set out to get, then he has been successful. But if he dies short of the goal of his quest, he will still have his reward from his Beloved.

Epilogue

In the name of Allah the Compassionate, the Merciful.

Hoping for the blessings of its author and seeking his sympathy, the copying and distribution of this blessed book were ordered by the doer of noble deeds, whose intentions are praiseworthy, and who calls for good [two illegible words] Bilāl Luṭfī Afandī, May He who is the initiator and repeater protect him.

I swear that this book is honorable. It is pearls of the sea whose uniqueness has been confirmed by consensus, who poured like the rivers of divine emanations, and who is for the spirits like rain for the lands, the undisputed Sultan of the Saints, who has unveiled the hidden truths. Despite its small size, this fine composition whose style of structure is innovative contains divine knowledge and Godly subtle gems of wisdom. They capture the heart and draw those who obtain them near to the holy presence of He who knows the unseen.

May Allah reward its author, the lion of the jungle, who has brought marvelous essences of the edifices and secret meanings, and who has subdued truths that are difficult to reach. He has borrowed from the light of Muhammad, so the lights from his lamp emanate and are sought after.

The publisher of this book in this land has indeed won. It was not in the possession of or sought by any individual. He has sound judgment and will have the fullest reward. He endowed the copying of the book using a corrected copy and spent on it, hoping for a reward from Allah and for it to be savings for him on the Day of Return. May Allah guide him to the best path and bless him in this world and the hereafter; He answers and hears, and He is near to the caller.

Prayer and peace be on our master Muhammad and his family and companions.

[Written] by the hand of its writer Sayyid ʿAbd Allah ʿAlawī [unclear].

References

Al-Dhahabī, Abū ʿAbd Allāh Shams al-Dīn. *Siyar A ʿlām al-Nubalā'*, edited by Shuʿaib al-Arna'ūṭ and Muḥammad Naʿīm al-ʿIrqsūsī, 23 vols, Beirut: Mu'assasat al-Risāla, 1996.

Al-Dhahabī, Abī ʿAbd Allāh Shams al-Dīn. *Tarīkh al-Islām wa-Wafiyyāt al-Mashāhīr wal-A ʿlām*, edited by ʿUmar Tadmurī, Vol. 39, Beirut: Dār al-Kitāb al-ʿArabī, 1996.

Al-Gaylānī, Jamāl al-Dīn. *Al-Shaikh ʿAbd al-Qādir al-Gaylānī: Ru'ya Tārīkhiyya Mu ʿāṣira*, Pittsburgh: Dār al-Fikr, 2011.

Al-Gaylānī, Jamāl al-Dīn. *Jughrāfiyyat al-Bāz al-Ashhab*, Fez: Al-Munaẓẓamma al-Maghribiyya Lil-Tarbiyya wal-Thaqāfa wal-ʿUlūm, 2014.

Al-Jīlānī, ʿAbd al-Qādir. *Purification of the Mind (Jilā' al-Khāṭir)*, edited by Shaikh Muḥammad al-Kasnazānī, translated by Shetha Al-Dargazelli and Louay Fatoohi, Birmingham: Luna Plena Publishing, 2008.

Al-Jīlānī, ʿAbd al-Qādir. *Fifteen Letters (Khamsata ʿAshara Maktūban)*, translated by Muhtar Holland, Florida: Al-Baz Publishing, 1997.

Al-Tāfidhī, Muḥammad. *Qalā'id al-Jāwāhir*, Egypt: Maṭbaʿat ʿAbd al-Ḥamīd Aḥmad Ḥanafī, 1356 H.

Kāmil Muṣṭafā al-Bālī (al-Ghazzī). *Nahr al-Dhahab fī Tārīkh Ḥalab*, Vol. 3, Alippo: Al-Maṭbaʿa al-Mārūniyya.

Louay Fatoohi. "The Concept of 'ladun' in the Qur'an," *http://www.quranicstudies.com/quran/the-*

concept-of-ladun-in-the-quran/,   accessed 29th/May/2014.

Warrām Bin Abī Firās. *Tanbīh al-Khawāṭir wa-Nuzhat al-Nawāẓir*, Tehran, 1309 H.

Lightning Source UK Ltd.
Milton Keynes UK
UKHW040823271219
355981UK00002B/335/P

9 781906 342203